Our Healthy Lunches

Healthy Living

This is my family.

Mom

Dad

Me

My brother

I stay healthy
with my family.
We like to
eat healthy food.

Look at this.

This is my healthy lunch.

Look at this.

This is my brother's lunch.

Look at this.

This is my dad's

healthy lunch.

This is my mom's healthy lunch.

Our lunches are healthy.

Are your lunches healthy?

16